French's Acting Edition No. 1596

A
CHARITY COMMITTEE

A Comedy for Nine Women

by

EDWARD KNOBLOCK

1s 6d net

AMUEL FRENCH LIMITED

A CHARITY COMMITTEE

A Comedy for Nine Women

by

EDWARD KNOBLOCK

SAMUEL FRENCH LIMITED
LONDON

SAMUEL FRENCH LTD
26 SOUTHAMPTON STREET, STRAND, LONDON, W.C.2

SAMUEL FRENCH INC.
25 WEST 45TH STREET, NEW YORK, U.S.A.
7623 SUNSET BOULEVARD, HOLLYWOOD 46, CAL.

SAMUEL FRENCH (CANADA) LTD
27 GRENVILLE STREET, TORONTO

SAMUEL FRENCH (AUSTRALIA) PTY LTD
159 FORBES STREET, SYDNEY

MADE AND PRINTED IN GREAT BRITAIN BY
BUTLER AND TANNER LTD, FROME AND LONDON
MADE IN ENGLAND

A CHARITY COMMITTEE

Played at the Irene Vanbrugh matinée at His Majesty's Theatre, Haymarket, on June 20th, 1938, before Her Majesty, the Queen.

MRS. ANDREWS	.	.	.	*Joyce Barbour.*
MISS BUCKLE .	.	.	.	*Athene Seyler.*
MRS. CLAVERING	.	.	.	*Gladys Cooper.*
LADY DARLINGTON .	.	.	.	*Edith Evans.*
COUNTESS FESTATICH	.	.	*Fritzi Massary.*
LADY FEATHERSTONHAUGH	.	.	*Grace Lane.*
MRS. GUSH .	.	.	.	*Angela Baddeley.*
MRS. HARRINGTON .	.	.	.	*Lilian Braithwaite.*
A MAID .	.	.	.	*Ann Casson.*

SCENE.—Mrs. Andrews's dining-room.

this play by
nce to—

.0.2,

' the fee, will
.ce.

ice has been

: issue of a

formance of
be obtained
:h Holborn,

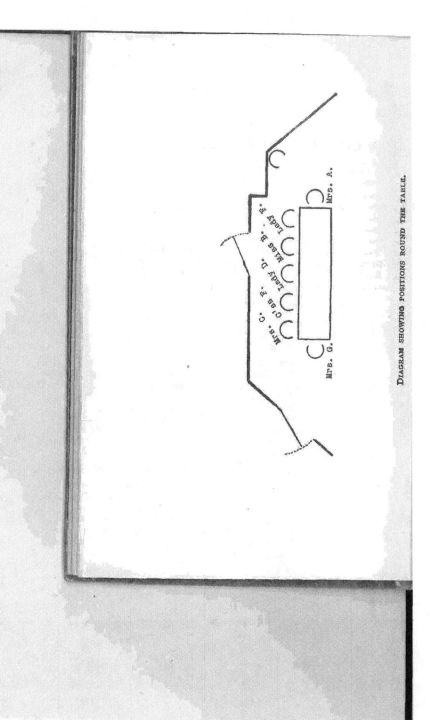

DIAGRAM SHOWING POSITIONS ROUND THE TABLE.

A CHARITY COMMITTEE

The SCENE *is a dining-room used as a Committee Room.*
A long table with five chairs at the back and one at
each end. A door R. *and another door back* L.C.

MRS. ANDREWS, *an " earnest " type of woman, enters*
L.C. *She comes down to* L. *end of the table, stops,*
looks at her wristwatch and murmurs : " Half-past !
Half-past ! Are they never coming ? "

A MAID *enters* R. *and announces* MISS BUCKLE.

MAID. Miss Buckle.

(MISS BUCKLE, *a frumpy female with an acid manner,*
enters R. *carrying a portable typewriter. The* MAID
retires.)

MRS. ANDREWS. Oh, it's you, Miss Buckle.
MISS BUCKLE (*crossing above the table*). Yes. It's
me or I—whichever you prefer.
MRS. ANDREWS. And you've brought your typewriter too.
MISS BUCKLE. I never attend any Committee
without it. (*She puts the typewriter on the table, second*
from L.) One must be businesslike. Now who else
is coming ?

(*She sits, takes the cover off the typewriter and gives it*
to MRS. ANDREWS.)

MRS. ANDREWS. Just Mrs. Clavering and myself.
(*She puts the cover on the chair up* L.)
MISS BUCKLE. And I—me—I.
MRS. ANDREWS (*down* L. *again*). But you are
merely acting as secretary, aren't you ? That's what
you suggested, didn't you, dear Miss Buckle ?

7

MISS BUCKLE. Yes. But, of course, I have ideas too, like anybody else.

MRS. ANDREWS. I know. But I've always found the more women are here on a Committee, the less is done. So I thought if Mrs. Clavering and I——

MISS BUCKLE. And I——

MRS. ANDREWS (*annoyed*). And *you*—yes——

(*The* MAID *enters* R. *and announces* MRS. CLAVERING.)

MAID. Mrs. Clavering.

(*Enter* MRS. CLAVERING, *a charming, gentle lady. The* MAID *retires.*)

MRS. CLAVERING. You *did* say half-past, didn't you ? (*She comes to* R. *of the table.*)

MRS. ANDREWS. I said three.

MRS. CLAVERING. My dear ! I *am* so sorry. The writing was rather difficult to——

MISS BUCKLE. I *typed* the postcards. (*She rises and looks for paper.*)

MRS. ANDREWS. You know Miss Buckle, of course.

MISS BUCKLE. We met over that Children's Charity—what a muddle !

MRS. CLAVERING (*nettled*). Muddle ? It wasn't a muddle, once I got it straightened out.

MISS BUCKLE. I thought *I* straightened it out. (*Fumbling with her typewriter.*) Is there any typing paper anywhere ?

MRS. ANDREWS. In the next room.

MISS BUCKLE. Not too practical, is it ? (*Going off.*) Machine here—paper there. We must reorganize.

(*She goes off up* L.C.)

MRS. CLAVERING. My dear ! Why on earth did you ask *that* woman !

(*Meeting* C. *below the table, they kiss.*)

MRS. ANDREWS. Economy, my dear. These professional organizers eat up all profits. Miss Buckle is doing it for nothing.

MRS. CLAVERING. What we'll save in money, we'll more than waste in time and trouble.

MRS. ANDREWS. We must snub her if she gets impossible. Two against one. (*She crosses* L.)

MRS. CLAVERING. Three.

MRS. ANDREWS. Three ? (*She stops.*)

MRS. CLAVERING. Well, I knew you wouldn't mind. I've asked Lady Darlington to join us.

MRS. ANDREWS. Not Daphne Darlington ? (*She sits at* L. *end of the table.*)

MRS. CLAVERING (*moving* R.). Oh, she's so full of beautiful ideas. I felt she'd be *such* a help.

MRS. ANDREWS. I thought we'd decided just to have the tiniest Committee.

MRS. CLAVERING. Then why did you set out all these chairs, my dear ? (*She sits at* R. *end above the table.*)

MRS. ANDREWS. That's my stupid maid. She always thinks that every charity begins with chairs.

(*The* MAID *enters* R. *and announces* LADY DAR-
LINGTON.)

MAID. Lady Darlington.

(*Enter* LADY DARLINGTON, *soulful, vague and mannered. The* MAID *retires.*)

LADY DARLINGTON (*crossing to* MRS. CLAVERING *and kissing her*). Here I am, my loves. (*To* MRS. ANDREWS.) So angelic of you to have asked me on the Committee. Do tell me, what is it all about ?

MRS. ANDREWS. Well, I'm not going to announce the purpose of it till the Committee actually sits.

LADY DARLINGTON (*leaning over* C. *chair*). How deliciously mysterious ! A charity just for charity's sake. How truly christian ! And how beautifully it fits in with my own scheme.

(MISS BUCKLE *re-enters with typing paper. She comes down to her chair again and sits.*)

MRS. ANDREWS. *Your* scheme ?

LADY DARLINGTON. Yes. (*She smiles at* MISS BUCKLE.) Somehow I felt your cause would be one on really big lines. That it would not be confined to one class or one country. So I've asked two most representative women to come and join us.

MRS. ANDREWS. Two ?

LADY DARLINGTON. One—an exquisite woman of the world. The Countess Festatich. (*She pronounces the name like a sneeze.*)

MRS. ANDREWS (*copying the sneeze*). Festatich ?

LADY DARLINGTON (*sitting c. above the table*). The name's quite unpronounceable. Hungarian, you know. She's in London at present.

(*Noise from typewriter.*)

I thought she could enlighten us as to the continental way of conducting charities.

MRS. ANDREWS. Really, my dear Daphne——

LADY DARLINGTON (*continuing unperturbed*). The other I have asked is a certain Mrs. Gush.

MRS. ANDREWS. Mrs. Gush ?

LADY DARLINGTON. My charwoman.

MRS. ANDREWS. You've asked your charwoman ?

LADY DARLINGTON. I thought it wise to get the point of view of the people—the square, unspoilt wisdom of mops and pails.

MRS. ANDREWS. A charwoman! And a Hungarian! On *this* Committee! To begin with, which of us speaks Hungarian ?

MISS BUCKLE. I used to play a Hungarian rhapsody before I dropped the piano.

MRS. ANDREWS. That'll be very useful, won't it ?

LADY DARLINGTON. The Countess Festatich—whatever it may be, speaks English quite beautifully.

(*The* MAID *enters* R. *and announces* COUNTESS FESTA-TICH.)

MAID (*with the same mispronunciation*). The Countess Festatich.

(*The* HUNGARIAN COUNTESS *enters. She is very smartly dressed. They all rise. The* MAID *retires.*)

uiles at MISS
would be one
be confined to
ked two most
n us.

ite woman of
The pronounces

Festatich ?
e table). The
ngarian, you

ie continental

)aphne——
turbed). The
Hush.

charwoman ?
se to get the
are, unspoilt

And a Hun-
n with, which

ngarian rhap-

ul, won't it ?
Festatich—
e beautifully.
NTESS FESTA-

iation). The

She is very
[AID *retires.)*

COUNTESS FESTATICH (*crossing* C. *below the table—with a charming accent*). I hope you will pardon me, madame. But Lady Darlington has insist on me to come. And I confess I have great desires to see how you arrange your charités in England.

MRS. ANDREWS (*meeting her* C. *and speaking with a bad French accent, pronouncing the " ch " hard as in the English* charmed). Charmée ! Charmée !

COUNTESS FESTATICH. And if I can be of service in my turn, ladies, I shall be very honoured.

(LADY DARLINGTON *beckons her to sit between her and* MRS. CLAVERING.)

MRS. ANDREWS (*at* L. *end of the table again*). Ladies ! I think we really must begin——

(*Silence is obtained.*)

Now, ladies, please. This Committee meets this afternoon to——

(*The* MAID *enters* R. *and announces* LADY FEATHERSTONHAUGH.)

MAID. Lady Featherstonhaugh.

(LADY FEATHERSTONHAUGH *enters. Very fashionable and with a superior manner. The* MAID *retires.*)

LADY FEATHERSTONHAUGH (*crossing* L. *to* MRS. ANDREWS). I'm sure there's been some mistake. I never got my letter to attend the Committee.

MRS. ANDREWS. I'm afraid no letter was sent, Lady Featherstonhaugh.

LADY FEATHERSTONHAUGH (*sitting in the* L. *end chair above the table*). Well, of course, that's too absurd, isn't it ? My name figures on every Committee, as you must know by now. There's not a single one that I'm not on. How are you, Mrs. Clavering—quite well ? I thought you were in the country ? . . .

(*They all start talking.*)

MRS. ANDREWS. I shall go mad !

MRS. CLAVERING (*from the other end of the table*). You must think me perfectly dreadful not to have answered that last note of yours, but—— (*etc.*)

LADY FEATHERSTONHAUGH (*shouting*). Oh no! Not at all! Not at all! I quite understood. I knew that if you didn't——

LADY DARLINGTON (*to the* COUNTESS). I think this is quite the most perfect Committee I've ever sat on. Especially now that you, dear Countess——

COUNTESS FESTATICH. I am certain they did not expect me, Lady Darlington. Your friend, Madame Andrews, looks a little angry on me——

} (*Together.*)

(MISS BUCKLE *rings the bell and they all stop talking.*)

MISS BUCKLE (*to* MRS. ANDREWS). I imagine you don't expect me to take down this chitter-chatter, dear Mrs. Andrews?

MRS. ANDREWS. It really is too bad of Mrs. Clavering. Nearly four o'clock and not a thing has been accomplished.

(*They all start talking again.* MRS. ANDREWS *rises and rings the bell. They stop.*)

Ladies! Ladies! Please — please — please. Time presses. We are all busy women. We must remember that. (*She sits.*)

LADY DARLINGTON. Yes. I know I had something to do this afternoon. Something most important. I've utterly forgotten what it is. It's gone— like a dream.

MRS. CLAVERING (*looking in her mirror*). And I, too, my dear. Isn't it maddening? This rush we live in nowadays.

LADY FEATHERSTONHAUGH. A Niagara, my dear. A perfect Niagara!

E
f⎞
y⎟
t⎟
.⎟
[⎟
1⎟
.⎬(*Together.*)
.⎟
-⎟
y⎟
1⎟
.⎟
b⎠

ll stop talk-

imagine you
tter-chatter,

ad of Mrs.
a thing has

DREWS *rises*
.)

ease. Time
aust remem-

: had some-
most import-
It's gone—

or). And I,
his rush we

a, my dear.

MRS. ANDREWS. Yes, yes, yes. Now first of all, who's to be chairman of this Committee?

LADY FEATHERSTONHAUGH. I'll be—with pleasure, Mrs. Andrews.

MRS. ANDREWS (*definitely—rising*). I beg your pardon. To begin with, you've not even been invited to join it, Lady Featherstonhaugh, so you can hardly be chairman. You see, this happens to be *my* particular pet charity.

MRS. CLAVERING (*rising*). I agree. If anybody is chairman, Mrs. Andrews should be.

LADY FEATHERSTONHAUGH (*rising*). If that was arranged from the first, what is the object of putting the question?

MRS. CLAVERING. But it *must* be put.

LADY DARLINGTON (*rising—politely bewildered*). No. I rather agree with Lady Featherstonhaugh. Questions should be felt—not put.

MISS BUCKLE (*rising*). They should be pronounced fearlessly and frankly.

COUNTESS FESTATICH. I do not comprehend your organization.

MRS. CLAVERING. Mrs. Andrews must be chairman of this charity.

COUNTESS FESTATICH (*rising*). You call a lady a chairman? Not a chairlady?

MISS BUCKLE. It was Mrs. Andrews's idea. This is *her* house, so this is *her* charity.

(*She motions them to sit. They do so.*)

MRS. ANDREWS. Well—it's exceedingly kind of you. I really didn't want to take on another thing this year. But seeing that you all insist——.

LADY FEATHERSTONHAUGH. I do *not* insist.

MISS BUCKLE. Oh yes!

MRS. CLAVERING. Please!

COUNTESS FESTATICH⎫
LADY DARLINGTON ⎬(*together*). You must.

ALL. We *do* insist.

MRS. ANDREWS. Then we'd better vote by the usual show of hands.

MISS BUCKLE. Yes. Do let's vote. Even in the Dark Ages I always wanted to vote. I was a suffragette, you know. I was arrested—just outside Buckingham Palace.

LADY FEATHERSTONHAUGH. How disloyal!

LADY DARLINGTON. But how exciting!

MRS. ANDREWS. Will you put the motion, Mrs. Clavering dear?

MRS. CLAVERING. What motion, my dear?

MRS. ANDREWS. About my being chairman.

MRS. CLAVERING. Certainly. (*She rises.*) Ladies——

LADY DARLINGTON. One moment. Are we a forum?

MRS. CLAVERING. A what?

LADY DARLINGTON. We have to be a forum to vote.

LADY FEATHERSTONHAUGH. You mean a quorum.

LADY DARLINGTON. Quorum or forum. It's one of the two, I know.

MRS. CLAVERING. Oh, it's a forum, I'm positive. (*She sits again.*)

LADY FEATHERSTONHAUGH. Quorum.

LADY DARLINGTON. Whichever it is, I know you have to have it when you want to vote. It's quite essential. (*She offers cigarettes.*)

MRS. CLAVERING. Why not do without it just for once?

(MISS BUCKLE *drops papers.*)

LADY FEATHERSTONHAUGH. It wouldn't be valid —illegal, in fact. Like being married without a licence.

COUNTESS FESTATICH. Some people *are*, you know.

MISS BUCKLE (*shocked*). How foreign! (*She bends down for papers.*)

MRS. ANDREWS. I'm sure we are a quorum. Anything over three is a quorum. I know it as a fact. My father was a Bank director.

vote by the

Even in the
was a suffra-
ust outside

loyal!
g!
notion, Mrs.

dear?
airman.
Ladies——
Are we a

a forum to

n a quorum.
a. It's one

'm positive.

I know you
It's quite

t it just for

't be valid
without a

, you know.
(She bends

um. Any-
t as a fact.

LADY DARLINGTON. Really! My people haven't had anything to do with money—for generations.

LADY FEATHERSTONHAUGH (*aside to* MRS. ANDREWS). No wonder she never pays her bills.

(*They all talk.*)

MRS. ANDREWS. Well, is it a vote? *Is it a vote?*

(*They all raise their hands except* MISS BUCKLE, *who is on her hands and knees under the table collecting papers.*)

It *is* a vote. I'm elected.

(*Feeble applause.*)

MISS BUCKLE (*rising up from behind the table*). But *I* did not vote. I didn't raise my hand.

MRS. CLAVERING. But you should have.

MISS BUCKLE. I was busy putting the paper in my typewriter.

MRS. ANDREWS. Well, we can't go back now.

(*They all talk quietly.*)

MISS BUCKLE. I wanted so much to vote. The last General Election I was down with the 'flu. And when I think that *I* as a suffragette——

(MRS. ANDREWS *rises and rings the bell. They stop talking.*)

MRS. ANDREWS. Silence! As chairman of the Committee I wish to state that I have received a letter from Her Royal Highness, most graciously wishing success to our undertaking. Let me read it to you.

LADY FEATHERSTONHAUGH (*rising*). And *I* have a splendid telegram. It's not for this Committee. But I *must* read it to you.

MRS. ANDREWS. Is it relevant, if it is not for this Committee?

LADY FEATHERSTONHAUGH. I have read it aloud at half a dozen committees and meetings. To the Little Mothers of the Motherless—To the Girl Guides of Greater Greenwich—To the Putney Parents of——

MRS. ANDREWS. But surely that can wait?

LADY FEATHERSTONHAUGH. No. I must read it *now*.

(MRS. ANDREWS *sits down very annoyed.*)

It's from the Flying Corps at Cape Town. From their Squadron Leader. "Tell the women of England that the airmen of South Africa——"

(*The* MAID *enters* R. *and announces* MRS. GUSH.)

MAID. Mrs. Gush.

(MRS. GUSH *enters. She is a typical charwoman, very Cockney, or any other dialect if preferred. She turns to* LADY DARLINGTON. *The* MAID *retires.*)

MRS. GUSH (*at* R. *end of the table*). I couldn't get 'ere before, my lady. My youngest—little 'Arold—he stuck a shoe-butting up 'is nose. I've 'ad the time o' my life gettin' it out.

LADY FEATHERSTONHAUGH (*reading*). "Tell the women of England——"

(MISS BUCKLE *is typing hard.*)

LADY DARLINGTON (*introducing* MRS. GUSH). Mrs. Gush . . . Do sit down, my good woman. (*She rises and crosses to* MRS. GUSH.)

(LADY FEATHERSTONHAUGH *sits down with a shrug of her shoulders.*)

MRS. GUSH. Oh, I couldn't sit down, my lady.

LADY DARLINGTON. Oh, but you must. We insist, don't we ? You're one of us. One of the women of England, aren't you ?

MRS. GUSH. I thought it was charring your ladyship wanted me for.

LADY DARLINGTON. Oh dear, no ! We want your opinion. Your point of view. (*She tries to make her sit.*)

MRS. GUSH. Well, I'd sooner stand for that, my lady. Honest I would. If I sat down with all them ladies, I'd—I'd get 'ot all over.

must read it

noyed.)

'own. From
men of Eng-
—"

RS. GUSH.)

rwoman, very
l. She turns
tires.)

couldn't get
ttle 'Arold—
, 'ad the time

"Tell the

l.)

GUSH). Mrs.
oman. (She

ith a shrug of

n, my lady.
ust. We in-
of the women

g your lady-

! We want
e tries to make

for that, my
with all them

LADY DARLINGTON (*crossing to sit again*). Isn't it tragic—the servility they still will show us. Centuries of serfdom! Now in Hungary—out in those great free open plains, Countess——

COUNTESS FESTATICH. In Hungary, dear lady—our organization——

(MRS. ANDREWS *rises and rings the bell.*)

MRS. ANDREWS. Do you mind, madam? We must get on.—The first thing I'd like to settle is where we're to have our next meeting.

LADY FEATHERSTONHAUGH. That ought to be the last thing to settle.

MRS. ANDREWS. I know. But I've let my house from Saturday for three months. (*She sits.*)

LADY DARLINGTON. Isn't she lucky!

MRS. CLAVERING. I would lend mine, but I have the painters in.

LADY DARLINGTON. How very odd! I've just had them out.

LADY FEATHERSTONHAUGH. I never lend my house for *anything*.

MISS BUCKLE. Being a single woman, I live in a teeny band-box.

MRS. CLAVERING. I think I know someone who will give us theirs.

MRS. ANDREWS. Who?

ALL. Yes, who?

MRS. CLAVERING. Until I ask them I don't feel I'm at liberty to mention names.

LADY FEATHERSTONHAUGH. But you'll *have* to—if we're to meet there.

LADY DARLINGTON. No! Don't make her tell us. There's beauty in mystery. Wonderful, wistful beauty. Just as there is in this Committee. We don't know *why* we're meeting. We don't know *where* we're meeting. We're like a band of blind and deaf in search of the Unknown! Could anything be more exquisitely romantic?

(All the ladies begin to talk to each other again. MRS. ANDREWS rings the bell again.)

MRS. ANDREWS. Silence ! Silence—*please* !

(There is silence.)

Now then—where are my notes ?—What have I done with that piece of paper ? Miss Buckle—did you take it ?

MISS BUCKLE (*indignantly*). Certainly not. I don't take papers.

MRS. CLAVERING. What was on it ?

MRS. ANDREWS. Everything in connection with this meeting. I'd spent hours over it.

(Everybody shuffles papers about. The COUNTESS scatters them recklessly right and left.)

LADY DARLINGTON. The greatest tragedy in life is to lose something inanimate. One feels it calling silently—somewhere, through the great void, in vain !

LADY FEATHERSTONHAUGH. I lost a silver fox last winter.

LADY DARLINGTON. Hunting ?

MISS BUCKLE. How ghastly !

LADY FEATHERSTONHAUGH. I thought I'd left it at someone's house—or in a shop. I advertised in half a dozen papers—but——

MRS. ANDREWS. I've got it !

LADY FEATHERSTONHAUGH (*eagerly*). My silver fox !

MRS. ANDREWS. No. My papers ! In my hand the whole time ! Well now—at last . . . We can begin——

(There is silence. They all take out glasses.)

MRS. GUSH (*to* LADY DARLINGTON). Beg pardon, m'lady ! 'Ow long do you wish me to stand 'ere, m'lady ?

LADY DARLINGTON. I don't wish you to stand at all, my good Mrs. Gush. I wish you to sit.

Mrs. Gush. I can't, m'lady, I can't reely. I keep thinkin' all the time of little 'Arold. Supposin' 'e's up to some other 'orrible game ?

(*They all talk.*)

Mrs. Andrews (*ringing the bell*). For the tenth time—Silence ! Now, if you'll all kindly keep quiet I'll at last divulge the purpose of this charity. Allow me to read a few words with regard to it. (*She rises and reads from her paper.*) "Ladies of the Committee, the object of this charity, which I am convinced will appeal to the hearts of you, one and all, is——"

(*Enter* Mrs. Harrington r., *a lady of commanding presence and voice. She is very agitated.*)

Mrs. Harrington (*coming to* r. *end of the table*). Ladies ! What on earth are you doing here ? You're wanted, every one of you, for the performance.

Mrs. Andrews. What performance ?

Mrs. Harrington. (see note below.) Didn't you get your notices ? Miss Buckle—you promised to send them.

Miss Buckle. I thought *you* were sending them, Mrs. Andrews.

Mrs. Clavering. This comes of asking an amateur to——

Mrs. Harrington. We're waiting ! They're holding up the performance. You're all appearing in that tableau—if I can get you there in time.

(Miss Buckle *packs up her typewriter.*)

Lady Darlington. I *knew* there was something ! I said so—didn't I ?

Mrs. Harrington. Otherwise we shall have to cut it out.

Lady Darlington (*rising and going* r.). No !

(Note.—Here mention the performance actually taking place, or some local charity or well-known attraction.)

Don't cut anything out. It sounds too horribly surgical. Come, dear Countess. Hurry! Hurry!

(*She goes off* R.)

COUNTESS FESTATICH (*rising*). Truly, I do not understand your English charities.

(*She follows* LADY DARLINGTON. MRS. CLAVERING *rises*.)

MRS. ANDREWS. Mrs. Clavering! You're not going to forsake me?

MRS. CLAVERING. I can't help it. I'm expected for the performance. (*She goes*.)

LADY FEATHERSTONHAUGH (*crossing* R.). It's really absurd the way people will mismanage these Committees.

(*She goes*.)

MRS. ANDREWS. It's all your fault, Miss Buckle.

MISS BUCKLE (*crossing* R.). My fault indeed! I took my instructions from you, Mrs. Andrews, and I——

MRS. HARRINGTON. Come, come! There is no time to argue.

MISS BUCKLE. Very well. Only don't count on my help again, *dear* Mrs. Andrews.

(*She goes off with her typewriter*.)

MRS. ANDREWS (*furiously to* MRS. HARRINGTON). I think it's perfectly disgraceful of you, Mrs. Harrington, to take away my entire Committee.

MRS. HARRINGTON (*crossing* R.). Don't blame me for that—blame the fatal attraction of ——*

(*She strides off*. MRS. ANDREWS *collapses at the table*.)

CURTAIN.

* (Here mention a name as indicated by note on page 19.)

Some London Productions
published in
FRENCH'S ACTING EDITION

BONAVENTURE
Charlotte Hastings

FIGURE OF FUN
André Roussin. Adapted by Arthur Macrae

THE HAPPIEST DAYS OF YOUR LIFE
John Dighton

HIS EXCELLENCY
Dorothy and Campbell Christie

THE HOLLOW
Agatha Christie

LACE ON HER PETTICOAT
Aimée Stuart

THE LYRIC REVUE
Arthur Macrae

THE MORTIMER TOUCH
Eric Linklater

POINT OF DEPARTURE
Jean Anouilh. Translated by Kitty Black

SEPTEMBER TIDE
Daphne du Maurier

UNDER THE SYCAMORE TREE
Samuel Spewack

YOUNG WIVES' TALE
Ronald Jeans

CPSIA information can be obtained
at www.ICGtesting.com
Printed in the USA
BVHW050156090223
658191BV00027B/820